# No Bedtime Stories of Soil

—————-

*No Bedtime Stories of Soil* is steeped in a rich lineage of urgency, candor, and weight. It is a love letter and an elegy, a plea and a call to order. The poems courageously examine the inheritance of grief, struggle, hope, and survival against oppression. Filled with unflinching fight, this collection is determined to see itself in the future, to press toward the possibility of sky when the soil is crumbling beneath our feet.

**—Suzi Q Smith, author of *A Gospel of Bones; Poems for the End of the World***

—————

*No Bedtime Stories of Soil* is a riveting assemblage that interrogates imperialism and its insidious offspring. Smith's debut collection is a stoic image-river beside decaying soil. What better mechanism than language to remind us that our duty as poets is to the people, not the page? What better way to chronicle these perilous conditions?

**—Daniel B. Summerhill, author of *Divine, Divine, Divine; Mausoleum of Flowers***

—————-

Smith's language begs to be read until breathless, each poem is an epic where the impact of the political and physical collapse upon a series of rotating images interlaced with current and past histories and lineages. Power asserts itself simultaneously from a multitude of automated machines and schemes, where the body is already paid and claimed as dead despite equally being alive. Smith acknowledges the many lived and layered experiences of this ever-present assault, while at times reorients a narrative of resilience towards healing for those left bewildered by the carceral, capitalist state. This first collection is a blazing debut, no one should miss.

**—Brandon Logans, author and poet**

In his debut, *No Bedtime Stories of Soil*, Landon Smith brings to the page what The Last Poets delivered to the stage. He writes with the prescience of Amiri Baraka as he explores polyrhythmic political themes with messages in his poetry akin to essays by James Baldwin, searing truths that force America to take a long hard look at herself. A reckoning. A eulogy. The last sermon on a crumbling mount. Smith's voice is the fire we need this time. In "Ode to Kalief", he writes "I hear you in the silence sometimes/The empty space between what your life should have been and what it became in the hollow space you were left to erode," signaling his collective hearing of the violent silencing of Black atrocities in histories past, present and approaching. Smith's voice is the clarion call for these shifted and shifting times—a beacon for what needs our most urgent attention. This book is the one we need right now. Primed for the kairos moment. The manual for next.

**—adrienne danyelle oliver, author, *the body has memories* and *collective madness***

Smith takes us to the afterlife and back, asking 'what does freedom truly mean and have you ever truly had it?' With words sharpened to interrogate the many faces of this global police state, *No Bedtime Stories of Soil* is a visceral dance with death and a call for Black liberation amidst a decomposing capitalist landscape. This collection is a roadmap through lineage and legacy; these poems are both a second burial and a love letter to a freer future.

**—Nia McAllister, poet, Public Programs Manager, Museum of the African Diaspora**

Landon Smith, poet, spoken word 'smith' is deeply contemplative. His extended complex metaphors re-embodies the lost circle of our diaspora's reasoning found in cracked mirrors, valued in sociopathic environments in which people are to live sane healthy lives. The audacity of his sarcasm brings to light the systemic covert treason against life. Smith's work is epic!

**—Tureeda Mikell, aka Mama T, Story Medicine Woman, author of *Synchronicity: The Oracle of Sun Medicine* and co-curator of the *Patrice Lumumba Anthology***

Landon Smith's poems place the pen perpendicular to the page and slice, with water and whetstone, truths drip and spill out. The personal is when the political been persecuting, a continuous tense kindling the words we need to hear– "might be time to wake up," – and asks, "How can I settle for symbolism when the core is still diseased" – and makes clear "Gaslights fueling mass explosions." Smith's poems are the blade and the blood, the root and the boost.

—Janice Lobo Sapigao, author of *microchips for millions*

*No Bedtime Stories of Soil* is Landon Smith in his truest form: an educator and a revolutionary, sitting between a book and a blade, he breathes resistance into the resistance; a poet who deconstructs "the contradiction of a white picket fence on a Chicago red line" and the "assassination of a Black Panther free enough to bleed on his own bedpost." He draws the horrors of reality with reality, an allegory bled to life with the crumpling of a two-dollar bill he held with his own hands. Landon takes us by the ear, walks us barefoot through a rose garden peppered with crushed glass, calling attention to every shard hanging from the broken window we see ourself through. This is a voice that heals; an ointment for colonial wounds.

—Antony Fangary, writer, artist, and educator

"Whether or not this "capitalist genocide called country" wants to admit it, liberation is the only way and *No Bedtime Stories of Soil* meets you where you are on the path towards it—be it as a beacon, an invitation, or a firebomb through the window of your most comforting fallacy. Part effigy of white supremacist capitalism, part ode to Black resistance and survival, Smith has crafted a thought-provoking, honest examination of the current state of Black radical thought."

—Meilani Clay, author of *and the creek don't rise*

# No Bedtime Stories of Soil

Landon Smith

BLACK FREIGHTER PRESS

First Edition, 1st Printing

ISBN 13: 978-1-955953-02-3

Cover Art: "No Bedtime Stories of Soil" by Cori Pillows

Black Freighter Press
San Francisco, California

https://www.blackfreighterpress.com/

# CONTENTS

For Amethyst Aurora Sierra

# PREPOSITIONS

Progeny of a preposition read to my closed casket.
I am running either
        to
or
        from
neocolonial pin pricks I cannot parry;
                Anxiety
                of Black folk watching Black folk fighting
           to make Black folk         visible
in a red tape bureaucracy never made to see this hue anyway
unless it's in a memorial service
filled with prepositions
        about
what Waller County framed her
        for
what trouble Sanford PD fabricated him to be
        in
The extension of red tape
        from
a casket
        to
a handcuff
        to
a broom
        to
the rug Libby Schaff sweeps lives
        under
                I am tired.
Don't have energy to carry grief, anxiety, and anger
let alone the white guilt progressives need alleviated
                I am tired.
Tired of being told the Marathon Continues
        by people who never cared about Nipsey
          His blood spilt onto the same asphalt
          I see in nightmares from a bed I wake
from
        only to not wake up

16

in
within cyclical horrors re-living
Breonna Taylor Botham Jean uncomforting comforter endings
                punctuated by my own blood on my own sheets


a coarse top soil or a cement solitary if I run too quickly
        into
this rage
exploding from the tears running
        down cheeks
            Tired of tears running
        down cheeks
        ensconced in red tape dangling from another participle on
                                another tree


Tired of preparing Black kids not to act as carefree as their white friends
since Cleveland slave patrol prepping bullets fired from squad car windows


Tired of "my heart is sad for you" messages switching prepositions
            to position another white person
                        atop their mound of thoughts and prayers
            not dismantling anything
Tired
of white women with cell phones
Tired
of breaking news
Tired of the prefix "The First Black..."
even in hollow celebration of distraction
in Calhoun Hall
to remind us "Slavery [was] a positive good"
Tired of concussions
        from breaking barriers colonizers placed then sold their presence as
                                God-made


White supremacy is an easy target
                            since it's the biggest target
Been shooting so long
                I have run out of bullets
                shaped like my sister's condolences

to watch me bleed onto grass to be the First Black something
                              First Black poet welcomed to the stage.
                         First Black man to die from the first shot.
                         First Black poet to write their own eulogy.
I am tired of these prepositions weighted with presuppositions
ready to kill us in dreams
only for us to die in our sheets
I am tired of it
                yet
                         it's not even safe to sleep.

## ONE SHACKLE FROM FREEDOM

I have circled the sun
again.
     I am well-traveled for a stationary target.
A contradictory colloquialism
     made into a breathing gun range silhouette
I feel the heartbeat in my lungs more closely now.
     The doctors say it's in my head.
     The therapist says it's in my body.
Still don't know how it feels
to let go of tension held
     in contradiction
Leaving me listening for a heartbeat in every breath
          every death.
     MD says I'm more prone to hypertension
     PhD says race is constructed socially
not biologically
Yet trauma flashbacks
     raid visions past lives made
     I do not breathe the same as I once did.
The price of opening eyes
     costs your peace
          We cannot go back.
          The lies are known now.

On a quest for a joy I have no map for.
I am one family tie from unraveling
into a reflection I have never known
     just to never be born
     just to only be seen as the pistol this tension has held up to me.
     I do not breathe the same as I once did.
          I am stardust
It was only a matter of time
     before the lives in my timeline,
martyred by destruction
     disrupted
breath stolen from a last gasp
breathed lost life into me
     The therapist says traumas are inherited intergenerationally.

I have visions of the breaths my body has never known
piecing together a past with breaths stolen before
they could become another rotation.


One
Jose Santos decision from not coming home
            Stolen breath transferred to a protest poster.
            Stolen breath read on a stenographer transcript.
                  Stolen breath just a memory.
            A forgotten afterthought.
A transaction in a gig economy with short attention span
Trying to discover freedom
            in a memory not my own
Pedaled to me on a plantation platform
while splinters infesting my feet
            just below the shackles
                  telling me
freedom is not life for me
                  here.
Even with this 13th decree
                  here –
Copper on my tastebuds
and infection from a neoliberal vision
splintered and sold to me
in a starlit constellation
seen from a triple-pane window with bars in my eyeline
      Dogwhistles transformed a plantation pipeline into a multi-story
                                                            dwelling

            dealing stock manipulation
      still transfixed on capturing freedom for some
restricting freedom for some
            never pulling splinters for some.
Freedom hasn't meant freedom
            since before auction block dreams transfixed on where and how
                                                            to run
toward a direction of hope
      in a faith manipulated to say faith is all it takes
so just believe in predestination
or is it free will to run

or is it faith in a


                                                       excuse me


A post-plantation post still screaming from the screams trying to break
                                                             free
toward a post-Civil War post reeking from colonized blood of
                                          indigenous, blood of the enslaved
fighting for freedom written by human traffickers
toward a post-reconstruction sharecropping post battling reconciliationist
                                          and emancipationist
visions against white supremacist visions only spelling free w h i t e
toward a great migration Harlem corner post overseeing segregationist
                                          tendencies birthing
renaissance's need feeding Baldwin expatriation
toward post-Reagan era posts about bootstraps and crack epidemics
                                          promulgating destruction of
reconstructed communities
toward post-Nixon post-Clinton war on drug posts smelling like
                                          mandatory minimums
and infatuation with Black criminalization
so please tell me:
        what does freedom truly mean and have you ever truly had it?


Coonin' for capital
Model minority trope construction just to highlight
the intentional destruction of my mobility
        but grant me the ability to punch a clock
        and I'm meant to be grateful for
                        the opportunity, huh,           'Suh?
Long as my tongue get that boot clean enough fo' ya, huh,     'Suh?
Shuck and jive for good graces
to not be placed on an auction block
with splinters gashing feet powering labor for empire;
        Corporatocracy
in search of an extra penny or two
        placed in a stock option
traded within a manipulated sanctum of criminality
        glorified in a Gordon Gecko Greed Is Good caricature

telling me exploitation is the dream
and freedom is the investment of a plantation crop
post-plantation stock
once a plantation block morphed into a share price.

Free to enlist as pawns in an imperialist machine
pedaling propaganda
about fighting for our freedoms
in schemes to profit from starting a war
with someone else
over the oil of somewhere else

echoing a blues song.

A Muddy Waters chorus capturing
the contradiction of a white picket fence
on a Chicago red line
drawn from the westside to a West Oakland assassination
of a Black Panther free enough to bleed on his own bedpost


post-Civil Rights
just free enough to fight for the right to die as a threat
buried beneath a COINTELPRO casefile
and a reminder about how splinters fester.

# COCKTAILS AND ROADBLOCKS

Back in this Hell again.

Intersection coated by lacquered paint
and salt of karen's tears bottled in molotov cocktails
thrown at any black person
attempting to walk down any road

                                        *Boom*

Better dive, nigger.
Try to dodge poison glass shattering
since this genocide project was built
on plantation bedroom ransom, too

                                        *Boom*

Better run, nigger.
Bob-cut lynch mob ready to wolf cry your dangling toes to stillness
Line streets to weaponize innocence
and turn you to property disposal

                                        *Boom*

Run, nigger, run!
Let's see who they believe.
And see if your degrees are made of Kevlar –

You can be valedictorian of
        You're Only Free to Die, Nigga University;

You can be famous, nigger!
Next viral open casket
meant to drown in news cycle

You thought that mask was meant to keep you safe, nigger?
Head of the class, nigger.
        Can't hear you beneath detonated tear ducts
held sacred by colonial torches to burn you, nigger.

Let's see if all that education made you white-woman proof
        See if you're worth more than this Molotov cocktail
                        more than tree fertilizer

        Flames dancing around your bones for sport.

## FOR THE WARRIOR IN AMETHYST AURORA SIERRA:

You have warrior in your lineage
  Coming from those who resist
  and Sengbe Pieh in your name
  carved into the dancing green spirits your mother prayed to.
F'thun etching into the world we hope to leave
  but doesn't exist
  yet
Breathe life into the community that built you
And don't be fooled thinkin' Black capitalism gon' save you
  Colonial tongues came up with spending power and threw
                  mythology
    on the fire for you to feed
    like the drone you are not
Tears on our skin
telling tales of how to deal with performance

Numbers might start dwindling soon
Not sure if enough tears are left
  for funeral marathons you may become numb to
Branches sacrificed for life to trace lineage on your roots

Great migration made family history on your skin
Never forget paths to Lapulapu's spear tip thrust into Magellan's last
                 breath

   Still fighting wars on the home front
Just trying to let time shift enough to funeral ash my remains
  Don't let me be the peace you couldn't breathe into
If air gets too heavy, pull your lineage from the smoke
  Dive into a healing before it's too late
  and you become all teeth
Before the world makes you share with strangers on playgrounds
Share pieces of you that do not replace easily.
  Make sure you find a way home

## KEEP WAKING UP ON THIS BUTCHER BLOCK

If you don't carve out a healing space
a legislator might use your flesh for sacrifice

Fascism fed farm-to-table
      Grassroots campaign can't rid the stench of shit in the soil
Recycled frame showed another Black woman with claw marks on
skin
      Gallery armed and ready for CIA to divide and conquer
      fiberglass bones to grass-fed beef
National Guard on bureaucrat speed dial
     *Tell them niggers not to loot*
     *or air fresheners gon' spill bloodstains on ready-made caskets*

Send condolences to another Black daughter
*Cut the check and tell 'em move on*

This settler colonial scheme can't farm-to-table your remains
      if it dissolves you first

Slaughterhouse silos with border bans
      and bodies of Black women sacrificed for collective white
                              comfort

We seen this script before
      yet y'all still ready to hold knives to Black arteries

Democracy just a fable we rode past
      crossing into this cemetery we wake up in on a loop
Until the shards of Black protest
      get beaten into another voter campaign
      for Obama to stand by a Black woman
      to wave clinking chains of Assata
      grinding bones into soil backed by Biden budgets
      and virtue signaling progress
      just to express-ship billyclubs

## THAT DOLLAR BEEN RED

Never had a dream within this colonial opiate
Capitalist othered a railroad worker
then Silk Road traded them for dirt

Threw a pig at a labor strike and watched bodies fall
Greasy palms lubricate prison pipelines while a moderate preaches reform
Property tax still funding school budgets
and they had the nerve to tell me grab a picket sign
while a rock sitting right here

Smoke and mirrors still breeding infighting over blood money

All money is blood money

Thought we made it out cotton fields
just to be grandfathered in
Heard a whip crack in a handcuff clasp
                    a sentencing hearing
                    a salary negotiation behind bulletproof plantation
                                                windows

Revolution on the verge if property starts asking questions
so you better step and fetch
                    or chant somethin' about change we can believe in

What we even doin'
before this next death anyway?
And why do my fingers still form prayer hands with muzzles?

## REAL BEGGARS MUST NOT BE BROKE

Outstretched hands with broken fingers
      trying to hold pride and pennies
           in corroded palms
      tattooed with trauma and shame
      shoveled atop
      triple broken backs
      bent over for false notions of exceptionalism
by socialized indifference
      unable to even hear change in change cups anymore
      unable to even hear pain in chain cuffs anymore

*Well I don't believe in handouts it's un-american so they should go get a job*
said the taxpayer bailout
      to the stimulus bailout
      to the hand-me-down nepotism / cronyism
           beneath bitter tongues
      caste tasteless from Covid super-spreader gatherings
      breathing numbness onto broken fingers
           trying to hold on to
           pride, pennies, and tent posts
      decimated by narcissistic neoliberal Eagle perches
           preaching defecation and meritocracy
      Blades positioned at the legs
           of those with hardened palms but
Every white business is a hand-me-down.

      Watching empathy disintegrate
      into sizzling pools smelling of gaslight disinformation
      piled atop hoard piles
      unused aside from perch positions
      and desecration of palms tattooed with trauma

Can't squeeze hope into a payment method
      of a profit addict
Descent deviating from a dialectic
      to a disfiguration of a toddler
      told their mother should have tried harder

Maybe the font on her sign was too wavy
        from clinching palms too long
        trying to hold pennies,
                pride,
                and enough breath beneath gaslights.

# CAN'T SCRUB CLEAN THE COLONIAL PROJECT

All cries for help fall on deaf ears if they go on long enough.
      Or if a capitalist can't see enough profit in the suffering.
What level of apocalypse hit half a million caskets
                         called conspiracy
and dumpster food guarded by capitol rioters?
      Ballot junkies backstepping on campaign promises
to rebrand imperialism as acceptable
and white supremacy as a breath of fresh air.
      Home is always the best place
      to find where liberation was stolen;
      if you can see past the smoke from headboard bullet holes
Compliant bones break just as easily if the CIA stages a coup on time
      Dirt beneath fingernails won't come clean
      with blood mixed in from bombed Iraqi remains

                  Maybe America was the broken home Gil was
                              coming from.

Oval Office regime changes
passing torches in ceremony over bodies

      Obedient notions of patriotism piled into squad cars
      to baton a protest into a senate bill's seat cushion

Colonial project just changing faces for conquest

# PUSHER MAN

Book said cure to anxiety was buying the next book
        Neighborhood pusher changed costumes on us overnight
      while pigs still scare tactic spines to breaking
Fearmongers fractured metacarpals for profit publication
              Can't let plebeians know power in numbers
Can't cure capitalism with neoliberal suture
                  sewing consumption into decimation strategies


      Every mistake is fatal so we shoot from second floor windows
      with no ink left in pen caps
Leeches preach on megaphones about colonial order only white people
                          agreed to -
      before assimilated white people agreed, too


      No victory in colonial framework
Enough blood sprayed on cement burial grounds to red planet this
                    project to destabilization
      Drug dealers in teacher unions
      and admin seat cushions
      coaxing coercion
      through conquest one anxious teen at a time
Maybe metacarpal fractures won't throb on bones cast as shapeable
Dry donations from board room cash hoards
      hoarding child labor as skills training
             Until hands grip M4s to kill Somalians for college credit


Neighborhood pusher camouflaged colonization as national pride


      Publisher plastered bullet holes with presidential headshots


      Told toddler to memorize warmongers for letter grades.


      Pasted letters on paper to hold liberation hostage


Might find scoliosis if coroner diagnose enough assimilation.
      Unmarked bills the only way out from pusher palms
        or cemetery dirt on a ransom note

# MIGHT BE TIME TO WAKE UP

Fell asleep in a revisionist history;

    Woke up in white apathy clouds

pummeling pandemic profits into a cotton field

I spotted Black men

falling in love with capitalism

between cigar smoke gaps

long as carrot stay visible /

long as chains don't cut ankle bone /

long as burning crosses hit the Little's lawn down the street instead


        Chopped my own hands off to avoid Zales globalism

        and wound up institutionalized anyway

No tears touch CIA tabletops when your bullet hole stops smoking,

so you might as well unclasp that tongue

before you become state-sponsored apologist

strapped to a Presidential handshake preachin' about proper channels

# THIS CITY SMELLS LIKE A MINT AND BAND AIDS

The soil has cried for so long
      that we can feel it in our bones when it's about to rain.
Arthritic Bienville joints drowning out minstrel songs 40 acres away
Cracks in my bones molded my hands into fists
         fists my great grandfather was rigamortised into
               atop red grass puddles.


      Had a nightmare about lumber in my face and wet leather on
                   my back.
        Woke up in a cold sweat
with my fist clenched
around a trauma someone passed on to me.


        my back ain't lighter
        and my bone ain't healed
           from yellow words city council painted on a
street
        with a redline in it.
How can I settle for symbolism when the core is still diseased
        Claimin' allyship fatigue got white folks tired before that
               Robin DiAngelo book
      even gets delivered


You will look at this blood for as long as I have to bleed,

A white wall in Portland gathering more attention
      than the pile of Black death they are said to be protecting;

I'm constantly in cold sweats
Looking into mirrors to mend stab wounds
      before they turn to broken shards squeezed in my child's hand
           Before they wake up in cold sweats about
                 nightmares
          masquerading in suits with shells
             underneath since


Every Oval Office resident is a war criminal.

Destabilization carved into pine and stained into white couches
overburdened by corruption since conception
Opiate addict trying to find meaning in a ballot.
        Breath in a bullet.
Reason in a microphone
broadcast to an empty room of empty souls

Body charred on a bed of upturned flag pins.
Maybe the yellow paint will sear asphalt long enough to watch the eulogy
      of a new 6-3 majority posing on Dred Scott bones
      Gavels beating the soul of my grandfather into submission.
Noisemaker on a Ruby Bridges strut sitting in high chairs now.
Noisemaker tantrums yelled into addendums now;

Silicon Valley nooses tied into eviction notices
      printed colorless to mask the mark left on a neck
to be criminalized for sidewalk pillow placement.
Yellow paint purchased by a house flipper
      turning lives upside down to paint over.

Still smellin' red grass puddles
      on my way to burn down a plantation before cement becomes
                  my last meal

## OXYMORONS LOOK LIKE BURIAL PLOTS

Margins filled with people cast aside but told to be the bigger person.
    Talking head declaring oxymoronic decrees
           lacquered onto policies passed
           under the cover of midnight amputations in
                hallways
           by sweaty palms pushing buttons
           afraid of what retaliation looks like.

Human traffickers formalized eugenics into government policy
      then distributed Turner Diaries to terrorists taking up arms
      against imaginary pyromaniacs
          empowered by poisoned police pyramids.

Not sure if we'll make it out of this future case study
          with lungs intact.
      Pandemic poisoning working class human sacrifices
      breathing toxic emissions from capitalist decimation
      Tear gas paid for by city budgets and tech company slush funds
      propping up genocide
      for stock options and public offering
Not sure if we'll make it out.
      A shack church glowing from a burning cross and a church
                bomb –
Down bottom death camps recycling rises to power for fearmongers
      Echoing in hallways from shuffling feet drowning out
      screams from            margins.
Oxymoronic existence ripping apart insides
           We have no body left.
All we are is an idea.
      An idea within a theory.
A theory with bullets and a constitution
written in tobacco tar,
      cotton pricks,
      and blood ink

Not sure if eugenics precedent can be pulled from tiled hallways
          and step n' fetch tap dance shoes.

Fatigue filling the lungs history erased.
Reservations about fighting for freedom
bathing in smallpox blankets.

# SUNDOWN TOWN

One death sentence from a hashtag list
      and mud slung at my name
      to justify the blood no longer in my heart.
Blood
      pulled from Louisiana evacuations and Mississippi passes of a
                              sundown town.
      Dreaming of a nightmare again,
          I tell my therapist.
Can't seem to leave trauma in a room
          I can't place.
      Sunken Place salutations to a Daniel Cameron shell with strings
                            tied to a sportcoat.
      I wonder
      if tap dance shoes still click after soul repossession
Can't seem to let go of ill will for the empty.
      Path forward crowded with corpses and sundown executions.
      Trying to discover the root of a sunset in a nightmare
          Hoping waking up means
burning fields
burning trusts
burning barriers to repossession
      and comment section Blackface

Yet I'm stuck breathing onto a Davy Crockett muzzle barrel
      before I escape from pointed hoods flashing luxury car
                              headlights

Premonition of my vigil absorbed by vigilante mauradery
      My grappling soul trying to know a smell other than cedar –
more flashbacks of lash marks for false claims after a sunset.
      Maybe candle light can burn through white smoke –
can't see clear path through nameless clouds of blow-breeze fascism
         hiding in a soiled flag bandana.

One sentence from another sentence
         on a hashtag list to be forgotten.
Maybe the blood on hardwood will

make the next generation fire resistant
White noise resistant
No breath left in a palpitation Woodrow Wilson
pummeled into a corner.
Gaslights fueling mass explosions
Whole country became a sundown town
under the cover of
Executive Orders and electoral opiates


Maybe my vigil will finally remove the tightness from my chest.


Don't force my breath amidst
white clouds and human tree swings.
I kick up origin myth dust
poisoning light for escape
ten feet from a Poplar tree border

## NO NORTH STAR THROUGH TEARGAS

Torn fibers
        spark outrage of ideology.
No North Star in the corner to look up to.
                Just bars.
There's blood in between.
One-sided fables became history
                      somehow.
My resilience you award means I had to endure you in the first place.
I can't be belittled and be the bigger person at the same time.
            We're all political prisoners –
                  some of us are just free-range.
Watching torn fibers tear into toddler tantrums absent of self-worth.
        Who are you without a knee on the neck?
Bars built into the fabric.
Shadowboxing leather goodbyes packed in soil –
Veils mask an early departure from crop dusted communities –
        Intentionally poisoned before the Chemtrails.
To be Black is to be a conspiracy anticipator.
        Uncovered another plot for extermination in the cereal box.
Kids don't stay innocent for long.
                Fireworks on the westside
        shattering sound barriers triggering trauma
        from triggers kids were never meant to see.

Convenient place for a freeway.

        Property tax discrimination written in the codes;
Sally Hemings' cries muted by the blueprint,
            I see red lines runnin'.
City plans pledged allegiance long before we were forced to.
            Stare at the fabric now.
Expendable products fighting to be immortal
        staring at stars that never existed in the first place.

        Don't stare too long.
Lines start to blur.

There's blood showing, now.
Cross-stitched tight enough to heroify pedophilic human traffickers
over a parchment signature
    declaring false truths.


    Definition of America found in the bottom of a Kool-Aid cup.
Guillotine bars brand patriotism to binary binders.
Folded triangles in slow motion meant to mean something other than
                                   empire.
I guess the orders followed abroad
        somehow freed my fingers domestically
        under surveillance by tear gas canisters
        and tanks crushing futures.


Control can't billyclub an IQ to silence –
beheading is the only option.


    Place your heart on your hand, now.
There's blood showing now.

## ODE TO KALIEF

Sometimes metal speaks too loudly from coffins.
Tales told under epitaphs
        soaking in tears
        lost from hands
        not strong enough
        to pull pain from your final decision –
tears too late to find softness on hardened cheeks
        and fist fractures severed beneath the innocence stolen from you
within walls serial in nature;
              I want you to know
              that I still see the softness in you
while the other part of me knows
this poem will never be enough –

to collect the pieces of yourself
left on solitary floors
              peppered with fabrication the guards tried
                            dressing you in
Sometimes,
we are not enough teeth for legacy strangleholds.
              I still taste your voice in mid-night breaths
              strangled by the peace you desperately sought in
                        bite of steel teeth
Wrought iron pressed on chests poverty can't press back –
Can't afford fistfights with empty charges and tipped scales;
              Survival was hard enough
              to pull the softness from you.
Nothing can be enough;
              This poem
              cannot be enough;
Yet here I sit with tears
in my chest
trying not to drown in the epitaph I never gave;
              Trying to sit
              with the memory I never had
              and can see so radiantly.
At times

I breathe from the pinewood holding your stillness.
Searching for answers in the haunting that wouldn't release you.

I hear you in the silence sometimes.
  The empty space

between what your life should have been

and what it became in the hollow space you were left to erode.
  The spots telling me to breathe after asking me to look away
and
I see your face in my tears sometimes
   hoping you feel softness again.
At times,
   I want to break my fists on the walls that pulled your peace from
               you
and left it in the beatings the lies bruised into your back;
   Feeling pinewood,
hoping that your eyes no longer hold the bars they left you noosed with.
    Vowing not to let history whisper your name in footnotes

## STRANGE FRUITVALE

Psychological warfare.
       Helicopter blades shouting you are being corralled
Curtailed and ensnared by the spiral of a spotlight
           to maintain that you are under the control of State
and peace does not smell air infected by spotlights
            and manhunts reek of plantation returns.
Property maintenance is the pursuit of badges forces.
       And sirens must beam dissent to jumpsuit window
                 vision.

Endless chains stretch barbwire yards to cotton thorns
          but the blood still spills the same.
Still hear the same pants from lungs trying to get free.
       Can't hear footstep tracks over tires
         jumping speedbumps to drag property to
             plantation porch.
Might find plantation post splinters in a helicopter blade
        patrol cutting through air over lead infected
                soil.

   Chase
       Chase.
Not enough Harriet in the legal pen to pull footsteps from spotlight.
     Each beam shone feels less chase and more bootprint.
     Warfare raging from whip lashes to siren songs.
           I sit with my nightmares beneath a
           backdrop of emptiness.
           Blood still saturating fingertips
           trying to touch something real
         built on rubber stamped retaliations;
Dried up dreams of the battered revolutionary
       smell like angel dust and conspiracy theories
    rotated in conversations with the same voice to validate the
               elasticity.
Bent into corporate slogans
     adopting language of resistance
        folded into the plexiglass high-rise meetings
          and ghost sessions.
Maybe whiteness stole its soul, too.

Or left it in a compost not to be collected before the second
                                                            comma.
                You know, a leech would pull your prints from a license
                                                            plate
                        to put you in a frame and register you as
                                            an offender
Remove your body from your voice
                Tell you it was your fault.
Boardrooms siphon funds from donations to two-comma contracts
                        still leaving those in need of dental work from asphalt
                                                            encounters.
Only bother with oversight
                    when helicopter blades cut through air above the
                                                        gerrymandered.
            Language of the movement buzzworded to destruction.
Might be time to adjust or become Bounty.
I run to the corner of rage
                    that smells like red paint and hands on lips.
Stepping on broken shards
                            cutting compassion in half each occurrence.
How many bars on windows did you see
                    fade to cul-de-sac on your way to a high rise?


Citizens United can't change you from a box to check
                    I guess I sit with my nightmares at a conference table,
                                                            now.
Delegates in suit nooses
                dangling from a PowerPoint
                        meant to wash off the red paint.


            Still trying to save soul from conference room
                                            addendums
                and mission statement masking tape


City council forums ignore outrage by agenda –
                Blackness reduced to another bullet point


                    buried beneath grips they never planned to
                                            loosen

hoping mission statements were enough;

One-off quotables happy to rebuild a status quo.
Casting nightmares in adopted language.
I'm just wondering who might be mural next.

## DON'T DIE ON THE LABOR LINE FOR
## PRE-PLANNED EULOGIES

Only fitting that a capitalist genocide called country
        be fifteen percent conspiracy theory
        Eighty five percent cash hoard

Drowning in hedge fund smoke
while television static sells dreams of trap doors

        Tells hurricane victims freedom means ability to die by monsoon

To die on the labor line and think there is no shackle
That squad cars are any less gang member
Playin two on two with black kids heads on squad car hoods

I still smell dried blood
on CIA funded accounts talking about Cuban freedom
                Talking about military intervention
                Talking about everything not talked about in
                                embargo deserts

Trying to survive redbaited strangleholds
sold as liberation and human rights

I still smell redacted ink on Che Guevara execution plans
Still smell day-old refuse on propaganda piles
fed to a future of scrollers and short attention spans

Fed to book burners in bonfire light
Sold dreams to loyalists of a surplus value
              screaming about billionaire manipulation
              screaming about cabal while
              screaming from deep corners of torn bedsheets

Selling capitalism on Guantanamo Bay bars
and Israeli bombs dropped on refugee camps
erasing tiny fingerprints from quaking headlines

# BE SURE TO CALL ME ANYTHING ELSE

Broke my back once and not sure for whom. But I know somebody made a profit from my marrow. Sold my spinal fluid for martini mix at gala cocktail parties. Didn't even bother to bury my body. Cremated it before a hashtag.

Breath on plexiglass watched my blood turn to ash. Then placed the next bet. Wondered when the next back would break even more entertainingly this time. Middle of the road megaphone ain't even hide the Billie Holiday chorus behind my stretched neck.

Butcher bought the axe for a bargain then sold the pieces to the lowest bidder. I come to you three steps lost. Trying to find a place to step back into a body stolen for sport. Stolen for jeers. Stolen for money lines and clouds of smoke.

Call me anything but bones when neckties start drooling lies from
bleeding colonizer lips
Call me Mende blade
Call me fishing boat rebellion
Call me the last three harvest crops
Call me Balanta warrior dance
Call me two Fulani braids

But don't forget to call the ashes ashes.

And the fire arson.

And embers the teeth of my last smile

## PUPPET SHOWS

Not sure if forearms prove fireproof on puppet stages.
Theoretical renditions of the same tale told in different facemasks.

      Hamilton box office dollars promoting
      colonization in Blackface and
I have
never been interested in the stage setting
of pre-written maintenance of supremacy we learned would not change
      I have never been a fan of puppet shows
        since they cancelled Fraggle Rock
      The last explosion separated another Brown face
                from an Obama drone
        sent from thousands of miles away
          thousands of times
projecting another puppet pushing buttons
for routine maintenance

The hands haven't shifted much.
      Other than telling who to say what
      in back rooms blinded by PAC streams
        and shuffled lobbying.
Ballot box blues tearing at consciences
      tied to voter suppression
        and gerrymandered patrol puppets.

      Bones broken for fingers
      to check boxes
      for admission to puppet shows.
Narrow avenues feeling restricting
      for the claustrophobia of Black folk
      fighting for a matchstick
        beneath a Truman Show sun

Jargon meant to pad the padlock
      of a straightjacket marionettes can't cut strings to
Another puppet talkin' 'bout usin' a voice
shouted into AFRICOM palms

## STRINGS ON DANIEL CAMERON'S SPORTCOAT

Sometimes,
      being propped up can relieve you of air     Daniel.
                  And what are you without breath?
What are you without the air in your lungs?
                  Perhaps you are dead already
Daniel
Body propped up for show
      to fabricate a ruse and
      the pedestal does not require any cerebral function
      at all
because
               perhaps you were dead already
               murdered beneath a blanket and an eyelid,
cast as just thinking differently while your breath is no longer even yours
—
      it is the pavement's
      it is the respirator's
      it is the fishhook's
that has pulled you
into a shadow of the self you never could be       Daniel
      before you were murdered beneath a blanket
            and told your thinking was critical.


      Pedestal puppet vacant of the oxygen
          that pale deserts have propped you up for
while your breath is not even yours       Daniel

         Can produce rampant rationalizations
     to eradicate the shit under the boot

Ashy lips preaching conversation as the means to provide air
for your poisoned tongue
               infecting Breonna Taylor memories
               with backroom handshakes.

     Let's air it out       Daniel
     Show the oldest trick in the plantation manual

Find out who pulled you into that Master bedroom
and told you there's only one way to get ahead
told you escape wasn't in your best interest
told you bedsheets only see color with No Knock
Warrants

The most elaborate ruse:
the puppet in Black skin with no breath.
Parrot to a whippin' post speech

The air up there is crisp for
a breathless corpse.
I hope you find your way home.
I hope you find your way home.
I hope you find your way back to life

# COMMODITIES

MK Ultra but in a classroom lecture about work ethic
     predated by a pledge of allegiance
     followed by an omission of guilt
     sequenced by a social service being cut to fatten Cayman
                                    accounts
               Profit propaganda
               funneling blistered feet on a slashed bus route
               toward payday loan storefronts
               drooling over which generation to shackle next

No time to grieve when sick leave is used up
Bereavement pay only lasts two days
     so shed that last tear but any more gets your pay docked

Commodified Hip Hop breeding Black capitalists in some shit
                   we don't even own
Sony boardrooms whiter than
     the publishing rights
     used to drive a one-hit wonder to overdose on individualism

Predators preying on products in studios
     and FAFSA apps saying just click that loan box

*Can't put a price on hard work*
*Can't put a price on degrees*

          Horatio Alger fables printed on check cashing windows

          Poverty must mean you ain't work hard enough

Hop back to job number three with a bullet in your leg
     so that landlord can passive income you to funeral service

If you die early
     you might balance their budget sheet for the quarter

Death benefit boosting production timelines

for tweens to accept fang scars on neck
                    to accept silver tongue saliva shots
Assimilation cost a capitalist less than your soul would

        Would give you a deal if you hand over both

Maybe materialism could fit community bones beneath Tesla tires
        Long as the charging station looks nice
        Long as speakers bump commodity loud enough
to praise purchases from Masters

Cuba been had cancer vaccines
yet capitalism seen as hero somehow
Padded pockets piling profits onto helipad escape plans

Preaching Forbes list aspiration as world service
                                as hard work
                                as three job grind culture
Don't let a token get you thrown underwater
        just to turn Columbus for coins

# MIRRORS

We watched a Lebanese building explode
        but didn't hear antiquity's screams muted
        in the detached ankles paving street curbs
as if
        the Nama and Herero don't whisper muted light
        from the misted shadows of genocide's grip
as if
        Dutch saliva doesn't claim South African neighborhoods
        dripping in miscegenation and curfewed cages
as if
        Belgian human zoos didn't barb wire Congolese flesh
        into product placement for silenced futures

We watched
        bombs fired into Palestinian bedtime stories
        beneath conflated narrative flyovers and timid teeth
                afraid to speak genocide to G4 gatherings atop sun-
                                                                    kissed corpses;

We watched
        Patrice Lumumba look into a camera lens
        before alphabet boy coups removed his life from breath
                        but did not see our own clipped feathers
                        in the falling striped sky

I wonder
        when bootprints will begin to feel heavy enough
        on separated soil
        on soot-stained appendages
        on epistemological carpentry
I wonder
        when the smell of blood will become the next product
        for globalization to share over viral circulation and knots.
As if there is another story of dirt to be tasted
        in the search of liberation
As if
        there is another bullet point to add to this list

that seems to keep building beneath bones,

> dust storms
> bodies
> torn tapestry
> choking hopes

scavenged for pocket scraps and power padding

We watched

from beneath baton swings and riot shield reflections
bracing for missiles and gaslights

from the same structures
replacing the same structures
with different colors behind sleight of hand

watching upside down coffin sagas

in twenty-four hour news cycles
scrambling for a next recycled retch

As if

we are not attached at the baton bruise

# ENEME

If you are enemy in a language you cannot speak,
      you might catch yourself writing hymns
            hummed before your assassination is called public
                      service

Have you kissing the landmine the CIA put at what used to be your
family tree
      Hoping you don't learn how to spell your real name

Chain names anchoring acceptance to a proper channel
          Proper channel flushing revolt
          down an oil pipeline Wells Fargo invested in
          with your direct deposit then said *your vote matters*

Minefield melting both consciousnesses
          waiting for collapse into an Invisible Man
          not knowing if you exist outside the language on the page

                          outside designated State authorized c
                            common core curriculum
                    you been enemy of
                      slave to
Shackled to petty bourgeoisie notions to transfer structure
      after
      France took your left thumb to debate Portugal holding your
      ankle bones to stand on Germany claiming your third and fifth
      vertebrae to make sure Dutch calluses don't beat Belgium to
      gripping the last uncolonized braincells not shackled
      to means of production just to tell you *you aint shit* in an English
      you thought you made yours from hand-me-down severed
      reality individualism buried you under for gold linens and a
      house in a white suburb

Thinkin' you can speak bourgeoisie fluent enough for neighbors to
                          exempt you from a
kidnapping at your front door if you keep your lawn manicured just
                          enough

Kidnap the soul you left
talkin' to the soul abject horrors stole
from that language you can't even speak
without speakin' theirs first

## JUDAS AND THE BLACK CASH COW

Toxic positivity said don't let them kill your flowers
        but Warner Bros. just came out with another cash cow
depicting assassination as hero
                in a garden with enough blood in the soil
                for genus to be renamed
                as reconditioned rendition
                killing flowers on balconies
        and in ballrooms
        and in bedrooms
        and in prison sentences
        and in public white opinion
just pushed for enough
        to *let those niggers sing and dance*
        *and tell their story for a penny or two*
*as long as liberation stays out of reach*
*and Black capitalism remains the only path to freedom*

        *Make sure they leave that anti-capitalist speech out of the movie*

Trying to discover a meditation in a COINTELPRO poisoning
           just long enough to know being twenty-one
           is old enough for a state sanctioned death
              old enough to have your story told in fifty years
                    as long as the profit margin tilts far
                        enough to the white

Still trying to sweet talk that florist, I see
Still trying to kumbayaa that garden to detoxify, I see

        Whose story gon' be plucked next
        from a loom of anti-capitalist liberation fighters
        decapitated in broad daylight
            to keep imperialism on track?

Black liberation just enough to celebrate life cut short

        as long as it's sure to be cut short

but long enough to cut checks to Warner Bros. and Amazon

execs

happy to *let those niggers tell their story*
as long as
self-actualization only speaks past tense
from carved busts and bottom lines


*And let those niggers coon on soundtracks about cash consumption*
*even if the Messiah knew poison when he saw it*
*just so they think Black capitalism is still enough to keep gardens*

*from toxins*

Just to have FBI bullet hole smoke put Judas premonition
three seats into the table
bleached to become solvent

# BACK ON THE BLOCK

When people started calling people a "Brand"
        that shoulda been the clue we were fucked.

Wait

        Then what about when Nickelodeon had a foot logo
        because the producer had a foot fetish

Wait

        Then what about when they marketed the Civil War
        as a war of Northern aggression

Wait

        Then what about pink and blue color association only changing
        for marketing after Hitler homosexual gas chambers

Wait

        That means
        if Bridgerton is a Shonda period piece
        I should be happy there's finally Black people here
        even if the lead is light-skinned
        and in love with a white woman
        and the only representation is

Wait

        Then that means that car insurance commercial using rap music
        and a Black and white couple gives the ok for rap music
        to be palatable
        or catchy
        or to whip that Nae Nae on TikTok

Wait

        Then that means social media is just
        an endless scroll of commercials

Wait

        Which means that big tech has created no surplus value

and a Marx dialectic is in order but

Wait

that means we are only selling ourselves
which means we are both auction block and auctioneer
which means we are both labor and un-living
which

Wait

that means we are Truman Show
which means only we are real
which means real is cold breath on coop slabs
which means it depends who markets their auction block best
which means we are two trips past enough in this litter box
which means we are the only extinction level event left
        praising Capitalism on a cross
        clamoring for de-regulation before we pass
        or the story disappears after 24 hours
        and we are back on the block

## MAYBE SHO'NUFF WAS ONTO SOMETHING

Call my body by its name and a torchlit finger might look down on you
     Tell you throw a label at me first
Play darts on my Black skin to make sure you see blood when label sticks
And don't hide that joy you get from my free fall
Non-Black hands still holding ropes to string me up for revenge porn

Crisis mediator said this is a safe space
      but I ain't found a truth yet in this graveyard
        project

Smiled and you called me arrogant
No smile and you called me aggressive
         Am I the meanest?
         Am I the baddest?

Just let me know where my grave plot lies
   in this gravesite built atop gravesites we're still uncovering

Anthropology lecture already reserved my bones as coursework for \
        Harlem excavation
Museum already claimed my Converse as permanent exhibit for boxed-in
         resistance
Dart marks still visible under red leather if you look close enough
Label tattooed on my bones for payback
Necrophilia drenched in the lesson they murdered me for

Make sure you say my name
before the glow gets rope fibered out of my skin

## TALL TALES AND THEORY UNDESTROYED

Potholes
        in paragraphs redacted
My neighbor still smells the gunpowder in the crops during harvest
        so she tells me be careful what I digest
Wonder if the mirror can even tell an image
        from its fiction this many iterations
            into a tall tale
centered around
           what?
      Pillows feel softer resting in an idea of pure produce  —
idea rooted in concrete beds blamed for concrete beds  —
      Maybe they should have tried harder,
      said the country not a country;
      said the hand not a hand, locked in a vault;
    afraid of its own image  —
Pastime book-burnings preached as moral pathways to salvation
      beneath simplicity
        binary
        dangling poplar feet.
Party tricks for border police on red lines
              state lines
              admission lines
              chain gang lines
*Do you wonder if we became too linear without minding the branches*
      said the hand not a hand to the country not a country
      but more dollar sign than delicacy.
How do you demolish a theory
    with a pulse and legs
    circumventing potholes?
Too busy suturing stab wounds with partial lineage.
Abolitionist cosplayers celebrating incarceration of the disfavored.
Must be ok to say one thing and do another
in a theory twelve times re-told over venomous feasts

# IMMORTAL

The dead can only speak through poem lines
So I suppose I'm immortal once again.

Caught between an ultimatum and a shovel
Trying to dig choice from surrender to ingestion

       Hearing voices again beneath clenching jaws and last words
       Couldn't discover remorse among
       the tooth necklaces and badges on shoulders.

I guess anybody can be a hero
       if the sky can't talk to the soil.
Maybe the liquor store can talk to the liquor store
       and tell where the rest of the bodies drowned.

If I die before this poem makes it to a panel rejection
Don't let them tear me from your clutches
Don't let them tell you I was only real in theory

I am only one line from tunnel light
Two lines from a rejection stamp
       stamped on my last will
Stuck in a fistfight using immortality
       like a cork board

Unable to trace lines to anything other than genocide Polaroids
and price tags hanging from a scythe.

Dead weight hollow in stanza caskets
                Wading twenty feet,
                   hoodie first.

## SOLITARY DISREGARD

Stab wounds
        dissolved to amnesia stitches
        and turned necks.
Not sure how often sanity gets found in cubic walls –
        somewhere lost in teased vision,
                    I'm sure.
        Right next to the pocket watch
        and the years lost attached to a chain;
I guess if the chain didn't rust,
                you wouldn't notice the life attached to it
        buried beneath a Tough on Crime speech
            from a podium rusting lives
                for poll numbers and ticket punches.
Confines became the best storytellers in a history
        bathed in blood and rust
        before repeated ablution and turned necks –
Blinking through decades
        pulling kids from carpets
onto construction contracts
            and GEO Group backroom deals doling dollar signs
        to bounty systems written into city ordinances
            and police union overtime clauses –
perhaps that pension ballooned when Kalief was unable to find peace in
                    cubic feet;
        Speculating where the
            time has to go before
        we find the discarded seconds
            for the bonuses and incentives –
Maybe we buried them beneath reward boards
            in teachers' classrooms
            preaching obedience for sticker placement
        and Pavlovian methods
I only know two places you have to ask to use the bathroom.

Cubic walls
        dissolving stab wounds behind teased vision
            and dreams of escape
        behind pleas

muted for mic checks on podiums.
Brick canopies building blockades to timestamps,
                    but I can still see the rusted chain attached.
Just enough orange on fingertips
                    reaching in folders
        for corporately crafted cages to put profits in the Black.
~~Do not~~ die on their watch and you will be legacy too.

# CARDBOARD BOXES

I witnessed a tear fall once behind a curtain of stoicism, hiding on a stage of emotions that didn't know how to play their roles. That tear fell into a well where repression won. Yet we all ended up here. At the same well. What coalition did our fathers attend that caused stoicism to be the default method of expression in order to "be strong" when you can't be strong; "toughen up" when you are too weak to know what tough means. Lost down a well only to feel nothing from never knowing how to feel.

I heard the medley made by my father and that became the soundtrack to an exposition I was not built to make yet. A medley of dismissal and "ok's" strung together with a thread of appeasement and minimization to the point where the voice told me it was more important to be right than to be empathetic. I do not know where the rest of my emotions went; Drowned in the bottom of a well of tears that never fell, hiding behind a curtain of reason – where it's safe.
Tears can be safety, too.

But I have to undo all of the suffocating done to provide me a route to say:

> I am overwhelmed
> I am indignant
> I am withdrawn
> I am inadequate
> I am helpless
> I feel
> I feel
> I think

But I was taught feeling can only be real if it is locked away behind stoicism. I have killed myself enough before I got here yet I did not recognize the headstones. Shells of what could have been; trying to revive drowning victims with the same pain they drowned in.

I have killed myself enough
I am barely here.

I write poems from
inside the shouts of a domestic dispute

heard from outside a closed bedroom door,
and conflict precludes exodus
so avoidance is channeled;
      I write poems
from a bunk bed still.
In a bedroom corner down the hall
from a caved in roof dripping rain onto mildew
Protecting my pen like parents shielding kids
from the weight of breadcrumbs and holes in socks.
Trapper Keeper notebooks filled with emotions I left estranged,
lost in a pager code letter
passed in class to another pony-tailed distraction
from holding on to lunch money;
        too broke to have emotions on clothes,
hiding being broke and broken
to not get made fun of for being broke.

My poems still avoid the thorns to not puncture inner tubes so I have a
place to escape when the fighting is too loud. I learned a pen can handle
conflict better than a mouth and vulnerability is pain. Logic is safe.
Anger is easy. A buried emotion is more legible than tears spilled onto a
notebook lines nobody gets to read,
      moth ball canopies
      burying moments
      buried in journals
      buried in wells of emotions
lost in poems I wish I could recover.

Masculinity is a prison; Black masculinity is solitary confinement. I write
poems from a father's tear that was made to toughen up; Poems from
inside a poem too convoluted to understand so they just sound angry
since that's the only emotion Black boys can show.

I am a poem inside a well. A poem inside the slam of a house phone
transferred into the rage of a star sixty-nine transferred to a tirade at a
front door about misconceptions of that white bitch calling and hanging
up. I am a calm built from the conflict of a poem on a page
written under Transformer comforters –

I write poems beneath a gaslight of feigned compassion uncoupled in front of a brick fireplace burying truths beneath starter logs and closed flues waiting to ignite from another Black woman being called crazy again by another man burying emotion behind manipulation again;

I write poems from inside cardboard tv boxes made into fortresses unable to be broken by a broke broken home then made water resistant to withstand tears for Artax unable to outrun the Nothing; I write poems from that swamp struggling to break free in a never-ending story about being stuck in a well Black man with minimal control over buttons pressed, locked in solitary; Stoicism is canonical for a pain bound by formula.

I want to write poems from anywhere but here.

# AN APOLOGY LETTER TO ATREYU

Craned necks from Blue Angel passovers and ice cream
                on my brother's face
        on days where summer warmth meant more than searches for
                                A/C units and cycled stagnation.
        Use that toothbrush, Joe would say.
        The lawnmower needed deep cleanings, too.
Boombox echoes down street acoustics and yardwork machinery
        Thumbtacks on cork board pinning snapshots to fragmentation
tied to red yarn and strained blinks of recollection.
                Searching for the laughter heard beneath piles of
                stones weighing down undampened snapshots.
        There were not always crumbled walls and monoliths.
There was light here, once.
There were ollies on carpet fiber
                and peg wheelies on asphalt
        after national geographic response letters,
                long before piles of breaths were lost to it.
Pull harder, I said.
        Artax deserves better than your giving up
        and
        giving in to the Nothing
while I cannot seem to pull memory hard enough with reigns myself.
Atreyu,
        I apologize.
There is laughter left in you somewhere beneath the sullied
                and yet, all we see is spots -
        pilling snapshots from lives tied;
And watching the Nothing take everything I thought this grip could hold
        beneath the smell of fiber tears and apple cider.
I was certain summer sunlight would remain warm beneath
                collapsed stone piles.
You were not weak, Atreyu.
I held you in the space of that cardboard box
        peeking through your pain
                entombing myself within my own.
Not seeing strings disappearing beyond recovery efforts
                and resuscitation from dead spaces in

The Nothing.
I did not hear you, Atreyu.
Somehow, you stayed left with the laughter and Moon Man spine breaks
were easier to slip than
I was able to see.
I strain like you and
I cannot seem to clean these sullied spaces with enough
toothbrush.
You were not weak, Atreyu.
Mud up to my grinding knees
keeps me from walking past the metal handrail on the right
just to find out I'm all that's left

# MENDE IN MY FULANI

I drag my Lineage
        through sandstorms
                dirt roads
Scraping knees on cement cinderblocks
             stacked in the way

My wrists cut deeply on the journey
             salt water stinging bones showing
             before someone else tells me I'm healed
                                        Tells me to move on
When I still grasp Lineage by their wrist
             trying to clean off eraser dust
             mixed with diamond flakes
             they sold back to me
        saying that's all our hands were good for

Losing limbs in mines
             within borders some European gave name to
                      that I should be proud of
                      that Sengbeh Pieh revolted to come back to

Maybe my wrist bleeds on the chains he broke
             just to be Spielberg'd in white saviorhood

I feel my Lineage weighted down
                    beneath Valongo Wharf remains
                  only unearthed for torch lightings or
                            medal ceremonies
Paved over
just to be paved over
    to be built atop
             under silk covers
             smelling like silence when sunrise burns crossed lines

Dragging Lineage to a native language
                  not a native language
                  in hopes of speaking with Lineage

between borders and sandstorms
I was told I didn't need to know

Enough Mende for struggle
        reaching past diamond mines
        mining through bloodlines
cut abrupt from Buckingham caste ceremony
beckoning Lineage too uncivil for breath

I drag Lineage with dislocated wrists
separated at the broken tree branch telling me stories in contradiction
to a tall tale pillared by monuments
and sand in my shoes

# MAYBE I ALWAYS KNEW LOVE

My mother showed me how to put on the cast iron attachment to
the middle of the stove so that I could learn how to make the perfect
pancake.

When I left to college, it took me two years to learn that they were twice
as fluffy as they should have been because I used one more egg than I
should have.

I think about my mother every time I make the perfect flip and the
underside has cooked evenly enough for me to want to send her a picture
so that she knows her hand is still on mine, like when aromas danced
their way down those hallways.

> I believed my father's sweet potatoes were magic.
> A trick on marbled stage. *I am here to admire*,
> I would think. Being trusted was too heavy a burden.
> So the day he taught me, I felt the weight.
> Like, this means something now.
>
> He spoke to me as he made them. Like his hands were now mine.
> And as I wrote down the recipe, I felt grandmommy's hand
> touch my shoulder. Whispering *welcome*.
>
> Bridging the cascading orifice between the generations unshared
> and holding me close enough for me to know what her love meant.
> To know that my father was now immortal.
>
> The first time I made them, I felt as if I should cry. But I
> was too excited that I had actually gotten it right the first
> time, like maybe I had spent years learning without
> knowing. Digesting the steps until they became a part of
> me.

Our house phone was in the kitchen. The cord hung long enough to
reach to the burners, if it needed to. My mother would speak to her
mother while adjusting the heat under the pot. "Ok, mama" she would
say for the fourth time. "If I get like that on the phone when I'm older,

just tell me to stop" she would say after hanging up the phone and walking over to check the cornbread in the oven.

Maybe my parents knew how to show they loved me in more than one way and I had spent too long focusing on the few times they did or didn't say or do the right thing, instead of the fact that they gave me a lifetime of recipes for immortality.

Maybe I knew love because I saw it before I tasted it; smelled it before I saw it; watched hands make love before my stomach knew why it tasted so good.

# GENERATIONS

My grandmother's hand said it would always be with me.

Told me if I didn't heal first, I would be teaching nightmares by the
morning.
Looking face-first in the well of my bloodline to see what not healing
leaves me.
When this rage balls fists in my sleep, holding onto damage sewn into
my spliced conscious
Fight trauma head on until my blood pressure puts me in the file they
red tag for Black folk

My mother's voice tells me she will always be with me and I cannot make
it up the steps bleeding like this.
Spilling trauma onto pages with questions ignored and spines snapped in
lecture halls just to
remain lock-lipped for couth
To murder spirit for assimilation and the promise of a maybe

Met a family before my last breath
Child told me there's only half of me showing
Said kids can see ghosts and asked me to find where the rest of me went.
Locked in a professor's bottom drawer beneath a story they stole just to
uncover more bullets.
Found ways to harm faster if healing stays out of reach.

Paint portraits of me out there, Grandma.

## AT LEAST PUT FLOWERS DOWN FIRST

Woke up ten times lost
unable to see past burning palm prints

Coroner can tell you jokes three minutes past America if you wait for it
Might diagnose you as rebel if you speak too loud about cause of death.

Every twenty minutes, another product dies by teleprompter
Tells a revolutionary to just vote if they want change

Tucks sheets in on deathbed for preparation

Hell, how you gon' make it out alive anyway?

Might as well laugh through that ash coating lungs
Used to breathe but now all we do is drink water and pray to the fire next
time

Burning flag flapping across a body someone claimed as illegal s
somewhere
Drew a border and said I dare you to cross
Let's see if you can take in more air than this bullet can take from you

First step is to tell you to dream
Second is to fall in love with a growling stomach
Third is put you on a postcard sacrificed to a tree branch

What good is the poet with no neck, the coroner will joke

Only half of half of the half he spoke to listened anyway
Burial plot center stage for encore viewing

# HERE || THERE

Perhaps I am still hanging from a rope somewhere
     and I do not have the wherewithal to see my own name
     memorialized in block and jar dirt.
Perhaps I am still aspirating in a dungeon somewhere
     in bewilderment, not ready to be dragged onto a boat
     somewhere for property maintenance
Perhaps I am pieces pieced together
     still tied to previous iterations screamed
     into these breaths I now take with reluctance
     to revisit visualizations
     knowing I am both here and
     in a rope
          in a dungeon
          in a chain anchor
     straddling a past-life and a half-life
          afraid to pass on pieces to any iteration of myself
     that does not understand that I am the breath
     in a train track execution as much as I am the
     voice of a classroom
Keep seeing headlights and torches blinding my resolve


I am afraid to breathe the air of the asphyxiated
     above dirt monument
     not knowing what the strength looks like to punch through time
                    lines


My therapist tells me I need to remember to breathe
     but perhaps I am still hanging
     still below ground
     still afraid of a future
          with no future beneath
               a future of museum boxes and
          breath on jars of dirt
I am unsure how to breathe in two places at once
     let alone three
     Reaching to hold my grandfather's hand one last time

before the sun rises and the morgue sells you that I did all this
to my own body

## COLLAPSING DECKS

The laughs of old black men
      can sound like gospel songs –
If time doesn't cut short the cast iron resolve of a sunlit smile.
   Smile feeling like home.
Home draped in choir gowns we all saw from half-obstructed views,
     fighting with the Sunday hats.
Flare is diametric in spliced perspective;
           we all get high.

First time I saw someone catch the Holy Ghost,
I questioned if God was real.
           Baptized in a gospel song;
      raised from the baptism onto a Velcro slab
trying to hang onto a semblance of hope
     in a smile only paired with gesticulation.
Distant relative of a building fund.
       I see the neighborhood done changed.
A lot of white faces hiding behind fences now.
Siren serenades are prelude to being triggered
      down
They drown out the gospel songs of old men laughing on porches
not safe from Darwinian megalomaniacies
underwritten in disclosures beneath the sewer lateral
         before the property
          tax gets lost.

Brave hearts always sing alone at first.
Fear feels worse than dying when resistance is a choice.
    Echoes of a rent strike falling on deaf ears of a
  landhoard
    to justify another cardboard sign on the corner
   Somewhere between here and Hell is where the money stays.
Tenderloin tourists stepping over homeless to document culture.
  It's only appetizing without the bones.
        Abandoned rooms smell of mold
     and dried tears before they're covered with primer;
Hardwood floors and indentations from empty prayer rituals
learned after donating to the building fund –
   penance for acceptance

while the laughs from stoops become inaudible.
Muted allyship caught on google maps surveillance
        scouting properties for free when joining a protest march
            I see the neighborhood done changed.
Street sweeping twice a month
can't clean the white supremacy cemented into the asphalt
        Don't hear decks creaking from Jessie n' 'eem's
            rockin' chairs much anymore.
Someone catch the Holy Ghost to heal
the dry mouths coughing in a food desert
Them floorboards been screamin' 1920's hymns on glowing lawns
and been warped for so long,
           it's just one more thing to ignore.
Protests are a family pastime for Black kids.
    Our trust fund: a protest poster.
        These conversations: an heirloom.
      Feared and held closely.

# BAREFOOT WALKS WITH A MELODY IN MY LEFT EAR


Conversations with apparitions are second nature
Demons take twice the time unless they're your own

Therapy chair holding my anxiety for a left arm
For the leg, I get to step barefoot into another cold silence

Hidden talent for catching ashes in my teeth
Found out every Black person had the same talent

Ghost of my drowned great uncle said revenge pays a price I can't get
back
while my fists clench watching a white person stick a smile in more land
next door.

Ghost of my great aunt's torn gown saying don't believe that lie used as
window dressing
You can whisper through amnesia if the moonlight obliges but you can
scream on your way down twenty-one stories and they would still blame
your tongue for noise so I send bullets back every chance I see

Put flame to plantation bed linens and let the fire sort it out
Water in my lungs will not save my demon souls anyway

Ghost of my captor watching diamonds roll between fingers before the
light goes dim from cast iron concussions
*Can't save a soul that's already severed,* I tell the next ghost

Can't whisper peace to blood memories when salt burns lungs still
Bones in my Afro beating drums for the arrival

# BALANTA IN MY LOUISIANA

Laid claim to Louisiana before I knew my coastal tie.
Halfway knowing where I'm from is new for me.
Woke up to Grandma singing to a credit scene up in Idlewild
Maybe I'm the time slippage
      between still dreaming and an ashtray
      generations apart


Dissolving into tropes
Deciding if I am my great grandfather's screams
      or if I am the grass fed by his last breath


I come to the river of my great grandmother's smile
      looking for a turning point
                not soaked in stories of untold grief
in conversations I was given through hand-me-downs
      wrapped in the branches from family trees used for switches
Hey, didn't they drag a body to a burial plot in these overalls?


Can't feel a palm dusted with addiction
      and coping mechanisms developed to thicken skin
                *in the heeeeeeat of the niiiiiiight*
meant to forget the cold bite of darkness
and ashtrays flung in moments behind closed doors
      and covered bruises


I am nothing more than a future Spike Lee script
      bathing in blood from paper cuts
      trying to discover direction somewhere
other than burial plots and tree branches


If they murder you in captions,
you were never alive here anyway.


Not everybody can heal through colonization in their last breaths
Never held hat blade of grass beneath my great grandfather's still heart
      that passed down forgiveness in the Louisiana that was stolen
                from me /

that they were stolen onto
that can't hear Idlewild TV set static
but can still point to the same darkness
where the bullet holes cast shadows over the river
I can't find a smile anywhere in this gravesite they tell me is a
country
Family history washed away to shorelines filled with bottles and silence
while I'm here trying to build a bridge
with blood-soaked grass and empty spaces
Can't learn a language my father doesn't know
My mother doesn't know of
My grandmother wasn't told
Maybe my dialect is less Criolu and more muffled pleas

## PUT YOUR PALMS ON THE RIVERBED

Told myself I control my emotions
        yet the seasons changed and pulled me from my palm
Set me down beneath a shedding tree and told me some parts need to die
if I'm ever going to grow again.
                Never spend time raking my
                own leaves so I'm sitting here
                suffocating in parts of me
                waiting to be passed on to a
                past prayer held inside
                my great grandmother's hallucination sitting on three
                                feet of

                nothing
I run from death on Saturday mornings just to tire out by Tuesday
enough for me to look it in the face Friday night and know I can avoid
it if I just run down broken alleyways until Saturday morning spins
mourning circles in my meditation pillow and I have to start all over and
act like I'm in balance
                Act like I'm two feet wading in Combahee River
                and can't see anything but starlight and fists
                since there is no time for mourning with wet feet
                        Only time to run
                        Time to get free or die wet and trying
                and death is no option I can face so
                I'm pulling on manilla folders trying to piece together
                              obituaries
                from my past life while Ms. Dawson in the fifth pew
                        back shouts

          **that baby been here before**
          on my way into the riverbed

# NO BEDTIME STORIES OF SOIL

Told that we are on even footing
        without checking the soil my
great grandfather was hate crime'd into.
            How much white wealth was grown
                    atop
                    his blood
in that soil telling me we are on equal footing without checking the PH
                                            first.
Forced extrication within
 the only nation birthed in a pool of racist capitalism
                still bathing in the fluids happily while telling me the
                                        water is fine.
Stipulations mixed into organisms easily denied.
                    Power structure complacency compartmentalized
            morality
sold in a firesale
        reigning ashes from trauma profiteers.
  Blood in the penmanship on scrolls behind fiberglass in museums now.
Written into the trauma
                cracked into the fractures of family lines
                I am not told outside of museum tours
            to not re-live horrors.
Who tells bedtime stories of trauma
        to kids in search of roots
                    fractured by frabjous accents dancing on the broken
                                    lines trampled
                                    by gun trades
            disguised as equal opportunity investment
or
            survival of the fittest
rather than
rigged implementation of dehumanization for the sake of sociopathic
wealth accumulation and joviality in amnesia.
                    White supremacy is a disease.
        Soil poisoned without allowing questioning of who's pouring —
Deeds signed in genocide ink later denied.
I got blood in my family line I haven't been shown

and mama says you have to know where you've been to know where you
                                                          can go
but I am tired of
                stepping over dead bodies left in the middle road in a
                                                          red summer
red state
            to fester as a promise of fractured lineage
                    and black holes in the space I will never
know because who tells bedtime stories of trauma?

Weighted guilt from balancing blaming my parents
                while not blaming my parents
                for not telling stories
of broken roots and poisoned pathways
to re-live blood showers they overcame
                        because
who wants to tell kids bedtime stories in blood pools?
        Whose lullaby rocks bassinets to genocide next to night lights meant
                                            to ward off monsters
        knowing monsters loom in gene pools of sociopathy
cast as patriotism brandishing gratified ignorance as a badge of honor?
Knife still six inches.
                No acknowledgement of the wound.
                    Mobility still opined as equal

Wonder what that land worth now.
Wonder how the blood lines mend now.

# Acknowledgments

"Poets are weird 'cause we don't let each other know how much we mean to each other until we're introducing one another." – Darius Simpson.

First of all, thank you to Tongo and Alie. Y'all worked with this vision from step one and I'm grateful for both Black Freighter Press and for y'all as revolutionary presences in my life.

Thank you to Eastside, Holla Back Poets Circle, and the Patrice Lumumba Writing Group – my degrees didn't make me this poet; y'all made this poet. Thank you, Christina, the best partner, for supporting me on this poetry journey from Mills to Holla Back to Litquake - and all the work that has gone along the way. Amethyst Aurora, you are everything those names stand for and one day, I hope you pick up this book and hold it with as much love with which I hold you. Thank you to my Mama for showing me early on what magic can happen when you can shine on stage, and for always being my biggest, proudest fan. Thank you to my sister, Alia, for buying me my first journal and showing me that writing down feelings and observations can mean something. Thank you to my best friend, Cindy, for educating with me and always being on this road with me. Thank you to Leon, Tyrone, and Trev for always supporting everything I do and pulling up to virtual readings – the Landon Smith Fan Club rolls deep. Thank you to my Dad for listening to my poetry and saying I remind you of Gil Scott Heron. Thank you to my therapist(s) for helping me be a better man and human, and, thus, a better poet. Thank you, Oakland.

This is getting long. I know. Bear with me. It's my first book.

Thank you, Darius, for checkin' my ideas with "thoughts and feelings" and always pushing me to be better for all of us.

Thank you to: Don, Nia, Monique, Meilani, Sarai, Mama T, Halima, Joy, Adrienne, James C., M'kala, Caitlin, Janice, Samantha, Antony, GP, Karla, Mahogany, Suzi, Ajuan.

Every single person who has made me a better poet, welcomed me onto a stage, vibed with me on a stage, pulled up to a poetry reading to support, took time to read a single poem of mine – whether I named you here or not – thank you.

And last but not least, thank you to every one of my family members, my lineage, and my ancestors who cannot pick up this book. Every single one, from Guinea-Bissau to Sierra Leone – one day, I'll come home.

To everyone who helped me get here: You mean the world to me and without you, there is no me. Let's keep going.

**Landon Smith** (he/him) is a father, a professor, a poet, half Mende and half Balanta & Fulani, the amethyst geode on your desk, Angela Davis' afro, Frantz Fanon's pocket notebook, Walter Rodney's fingernail, the 7-10 bowling split, your favorite pillow.

Despite his institutional degrees, he really became a poet through the East Side Arts Alliance in Oakland. Landon thanks his sister Alia for buying him his first journal, Brit Hill for pushing him to read poetry in public, and Black Freighter press for publishing his first book - No Bedtime Stories of Soil. Abolish all prisons and police.

"There's a ship
The Black Freighter
With a skull on it's masthead
Will be coming in"


— Nina Simone, Pirate Jenny


**Black Freighter Press** publishes revolutionary books. committed to the exploration of liberation, using art to transform consciousness. A platform for Black and Brown writers to honor ancestry and propel radical imagination.